Terms and Conditions

LEGAL NOTICE

The Publisher has strived to be as accurate and complete as possible in the creation of this report, notwithstanding the fact that he does not warrant or represent at any time that the contents within are accurate due to the rapidly changing nature of the Internet.

While all attempts have been made to verify information provided in this publication, the Publisher assumes no responsibility for errors, omissions, or contrary interpretation of the subject matter herein. Any perceived slights of specific persons, peoples, or organizations are unintentional.

In practical advice books, like anything else in life, there are no guarantees of income made. Readers are cautioned to reply on their own judgment about their individual circumstances to act accordingly.

This book is not intended for use as a source of legal, business, accounting or financial advice. All readers are advised to seek services of competent professionals in legal, business, accounting and finance fields.

You are encouraged to print this book for easy reading.

Table Of Contents

Foreword

Chapter 1:
The Benefits Of Audio Products

Chapter 2:
Choosing Your PLR Topic For Your Product

Chapter 3:
How Will you Use Your Audio Product

Chapter 4:
Presenting The Product

Chapter 5:
Get The Correct Tools

Chapter 6:
Create The Transcript From PLR

Wrapping Up

Foreword

Audio products are ultra- hot and on the rise. Just about everybody has an iPod or MP3 player today. With a couple of clicks anybody may buy an audio product, upload it to their iPod or MP3 player and listen to it as they set about their day.

Discover you a few really great PLR products and begin producing audio products. Or you can make audio products from scratch. Here we will explore how to accomplish this.

How To Create An Audio Product To Sell For Clickbank

Chapter 1:
The Benefits Of Audio Products

Synopsis

Adding audio to your site or blog or producing an audio product for Clickbank is an efficient way to draw in more visitors. It goes without saying that audio truly supplies a fresh communication technique significantly diversifying your current product offers as well as promotion tools. Put differently it plainly motivates purchases.

There are a lot of ways audio may truly help to motivate purchases. So let me illustrate them here.

The Advantages

First off you ought to understand that audio material is among the best ways to introduce your personality to your likely buyers. With great audio material it will be simple to communicate to your audience. In that case you'll have no troubles with targeting your market group.

By merely listening to you, individuals will be able to perceive you as a true human. Consequently they'll likely become your customers and a lot of studies demonstrate it. You ought to actively utilize audio messages to touch base with your targeted audience and this will have a great affect on them. Incidentally even a simple welcome message can be a perfect start.

Audio may promote you as a true authority in your field. As usual individuals buy things from individuals and companies they truly consider to be a real expert or authority in their specific industry. Audio is a mighty tool enabling you to exhibit your authority on your niche. This way you'll be able to supply extended info to your potential buyers in a short time period. Professionals know for certain that even 5 minutes of listening to your message will greatly influence your buyers.

Audio material is able to add proof. I ought to say that individuals frequently make their purchasing decisions being prompted by the opinions of others. Incidentally it's called social proof. So this social proof is particularly crucial if these advisers are those people your target market truly respects. If you truly wish to capitalize on this social proof then you ought to simply interview some experts in your field and then place audio testimonials on your web site.

mandatory for the marketing industry to promote online, where individuals are.

Audio Ads is a radical way to make all of this occur while likewise keeping the buyers satisfied instead of feeling invaded by ads.

DVRs are a different factor in why advertising and marketing have to shift drastically. 33.5 million individuals will have DVRs in their homes soon and over 90% of the individuals who already own them claim that they fast forward through ads.

They likewise claim that it's a relief not to have to view them unless the commercial has been given a report for being particularly engaging.

Before long there won't be a reason at all to exhibit commercials on TV or cable unless their writers may pump out their most amazing work every single time a company wishes to display a new ad.

The fact that there's a lack of interaction in TV is simply further proof that Net is the way of the future. Youngsters and teens are less interested in watching others (actors) live out the lives that everybody wishes they had.

Rather they're playing interactive games and shows and living out the illusion lives that they wish.

YouTube has likewise played a large role in how entertainment is shifting too. Individuals who used to be intrigued with shows like America's Funniest Videos are now viewing them on YouTube, commercial free.

What are audio ads?

Audio advertisements are a way for marketers to promote their products to individuals on related sites with 5-30 second audio clips.

Like Google Adwords, the marketers will view a list of sites that wish to add related ads to their site for payment. They'll then bid on the best sites for the ads they wish to run and when the bid is won, the ad is then embedded into the language of the site owner.

Audio advertisements also may run like Adsense. The visitor or viewer doesn't need to click on anything in order for the ad to be activated.

The ads are sound only and they only last for 5-30 seconds. They're not like pop up ads.

Rather, they're audio tracks that mechanically play when an individual views a certain site or page. What's so amazing about this, besides that it's only 5-30 seconds long is that the ad is associated to the content on that page.

For instance, if a visitor was visiting Sue's intimate apparel online, the audio ad that may play for that visitor would be a 5-30 second message for XYZ bras. It's brilliance.

Who do audio advertisements benefit?

Although many of the audio ads that presently run are for big corporations like Taco Bell, small site owners may benefit from this program also.

As a matter of fact, the advantages are at both ends as marketers and little business owners who battle to pay for their cable ads will find these systems much more affordable.

Those who were not able to afford any ad at all might now be able to advertise on the net.

Learning With Audio

Books on tapes, audio books, and additional audio learning devices are quickly acquiring popularity in the instruction field. In utilizing audio books for the aim of education, people are relieved that its advantages are many.

The increasing success of beginning and struggling readers is frequently credited to utilizing audio books as part of their studying process. Apart from this, there are additional benefits in utilizing audio materials not only in schools, but likewise in homes and other places.

There's no refusing the fact that most individuals hated reading as youngsters. Only some people enjoy reading, particularly if there's an alternative.

Audio books have today made it possible for people to get better access to content that they don't like reading.

Experts have agreed that audio books go a long way to help people more than conventional books, particularly for those who have difficulty in reading.

Below are some particular advantages of utilizing audio books:

Utilizing audio books to teach people provides them "assortment".

There are particular audio books made that are not only educative but really entertaining. These sorts of audio books make learning much more fun.

For people with reading difficulties, they may slowly follow the readings from audio books till it feels comfortable to read.

Merely following an audio book while viewing the printed material in front of them, may increase their learning skills by a really high percentage.

Audio books save cash. Rather than buying dozens of books for a lesson, just one audio book may be played for all concerned.

Audio books that tell intriguing stories are really helpful in times when people have become too tired to read and study.

People may not particularly love printed books as much as they do audio books. It feels much easier for them to "listen" to an audio book than "read" a book.

Altogether, most people find it a good deal of fun listening to a lesson on audio, instead of having to read it. That's why people spend a lot of time watching movies, instead of reading.

Chapter 2:

Choosing Your PLR Topic For Your Product

Synopsis

The beginning thing you need to do is decide what issue you'll be producing your audio products around. Do your research. Visit some forums and see what individuals are talking about. Study a lot of different publications. Do keyword research and work out what individuals are searching for.

When you've discovered a topic you wish to utilize for your audio product begin looking for additional info you are able to add. By adding different sorts of PLR products you're producing a unique product that is not available anyplace else.

Getting The Product Started

Choosing an audio product topic is a little more difficult than choosing a general subject, as you have the additional dimension of sound. Not only does your audio require some kind of substance, but you have to conceive of how you're going to record it, how you're going to edit it, what sort of sound you're going for.

Individuals, in virtually every corner of the Earth, require answers to their troubles and these same individuals are going online to attempt and discover these answers. The Net has produced the world's biggest knowledge database where individuals will look for info.

Why would individuals wish to purchase something?

These individuals have troubles; a few real, a few imaginary, and these may only be solved when somebody like you supplies the necessary info they require. This info may be provided in the form of a unique info product produced from PLR material.

What product area, or niche, ought you work on?

All the same, before you are able to sell any sort of product, info based or otherwise, you have to first choose what sort of niche you plan to work on. Think of this, a niche is nothing more than a particular class, or area of concern. It's a selected area of concern which you'll have explored to make certain there's sufficient demand for a remedy to a perceived issue.

There's no point in spending hours producing a marketing plan and making a brilliant product if, at the close of it all, no-one really has any need for your product. Your selected product, in your selected niche, has to address an issue that individuals need to remedy.

How do you recognize what individuals require? – Discovering themes for your niche.

Prior to you do anything you'll initially have to carry on some niche research to discover what individuals are seeking on the net. Without this crucial step, you're likely to bomb as you'd be producing a product without knowing whether there's a requirement for it or not. You can't simply jump into a business and trust for the best.

As luck would have it, you don't have to enter the market blind. You are able to learn everything you have to know about assembling a profitable product by conducting a little research on the internet. Most individuals avoid the research stage but this is an error. You are able to conduct research simply using a couple of easy techniques. You never know, it may even be amusing.

You have to accomplish the research as not every niche will make income. That's simply the way it is. Without the research, there's a solid chance you'll choose a niche that doesn't work.

Selecting your niche.

One crucial point to start with, when you set about your research it's crucial that as you discover matters that interest you, keep a notation of them whether you plan to utilize them right away or not. That's

because you might discover something now that you're intrigued in but it doesn't have a big market but that might shift in a couple of years. This way, you'll constantly have a file of niche themes you are able to go back to when you require to come up with new products.

Here are the 2 chief steps you ought to follow when exploring a

niche: Brainstorming

You'll do this to muster up a list of themes for niche subjects you wish to research. Come up with as many themes about niche categories as you are able to. When producing your list, recall there are differences between what a "subject" is and what a "niche" is. For example, let's suppose you come up with the theme of candles. Candles are a basic topic. Aromatherapy candles nevertheless, are a niche theme. Lilac aromatherapy therapeutic candles is even more niche. Do you realize the difference? While doing your research, you'll discover a lot of topics. Plow ahead and put them all down, then advance to the next step.

Make your list as exact as imaginable.

Following, specify your list, making it as exact as imaginable. You need to choose the best niche product classes, the ones that will make you the most cash and the ones you've an interest in. Don't pick out a niche category simply because you're likely to make income. Choose one that will let you make income, but one you likewise have a passion for. You're much more probable to commit your time and energy to a project if you're passionate about it.

These 2 steps will supply a focus for when you come to select the products that you would like to be involved with. Remember, what individuals require is a solution to an issue and not the actual product itself.

Additional Tips

Make sure you consider what you're passionate about. Products can take a lot of time, energy, and manpower to make, and particularly if you're starting up and can't pay individuals a lot of money to work for you, you have to go with an issue that you're passionate about and you believe in. When you come up with these subjects, consider how these subjects may be told with audio. What makes the topic tributary to audio, and why would individuals appreciate hearing it, as opposed to reading about it.

Decide what your goals are. What are you skills, and what do you desire to bring to the public? Are you making this product to enhance the material of a web site that you already run?

Consider your audience. Who are you targeting?

Consider how often you have to create products and how you'd organize it. Can you see this audio topic keeping individual's attention for a while? First and foremost, can you see it keeping you energized for a while?

Chapter 3:
How Will you Use Your Audio Product

Synopsis

The following thing you need to do is work out how you'll utilize your audio product. Do you wish to sell it as a digital audio product? Do you wish to give it away as a list builder? Do you wish to provide it as a tangible product or a front end product?

Decide The Purpose

Let's view these in additional detail:

Sell it as digital or tangible product on Clickbank - An audio product has a worth much more gravid than a regular eBook. The ordinary price of an eBook today is approximately twenty-seven bucks. That same twenty-seven dollar eBook may sell for approximately $67 as a digital audio product or perhaps even $97 as a tangible audio product.

You are able to make at least $40 more simply by placing in a bit of additional work. If you wish to be able to reach a much fuller audience then think about offering your product as both an eBook edition and an audio edition.

This is among the most originative techniques you are able to apply it to make cash with no list and likewise almost completely annihilate all rivals. The goal is to discover products that are already selling and then providing premium versions of the same products. This commonly means providing the same product in audio format. Individuals learn in different formats, and a greater percentage of your buyers will prefer hearing over reading to consume the content.

Over 38% of your target markets favor learning thru audio over reading.

How do you capitalize on this? Easy. A chief benefit that works in your favor is that individuals are willing to pay premium pricing for the same information when it's delivered thru audio. For instance, the audio version of a bestselling eBook will sell for 4-10 times the pilot price of the book.

Here's one way to use this technique:

Travel to Clickbank and distinguish the top ten selling products in Clickbank in a category you're concerned with, but might not be an authority in. Then, put down the contact info of every product creator: get the number, if there's one available.

The tilt is this: you are able to provide a % of the premium product for every sale that's made, and that's yet more what the product owner would bring in when he sells one copy of his present downloadable product. As an illustration, let's presume that you discover a bestselling eBook on stock certificate trading.

Get hold of the product owner and tell him you'd like to sell a premium edition of his book as a percentage of his existing buyers favor learning thru audio.

By pre-selling the premium product to the list possessor, you'll get prepaid and you are able to utilize those funds to produce the premium product. In many cases, you are able to do the bulk of the work yourself utilizing low-cost tools readily usable on the Net.

If presented the right way, most product owners are hospitable to this as it helps them to produce cash without having to do additional work. Additionally, they may now show their buyers that they care because they're providing them a premium edition of a product that has been demonstrated to sell. Additionally, this technique capitalizes on all the affiliates that the list possessor already has in place and spares you the bother of producing your own affiliate program.

Your conversion rate will be a great deal higher as you're being backed by the list possessor and in most instances, there's a repressed demand for higher-end products that the list possessor hasn't fulfilled. Many list possessors gravely underestimate their buyers' ability to consume products and quit selling too early or not enough.

You don't need to limit yourself to Clickbank: you are able to repeat this same technique with the Amazon Best Seller list or any additional best seller list. The key is that you are adopting someone else's credibility to immediately launch a product to a market that's already demonstrated to purchase.

Give it away for free as a list establisher - gratis giveaways are a way to establish any list. Give your likely buyers a quality informative audio product in exchange for their name and e-mail address. Give them merely enough to make them wish to return for more.

Utilize it as a front end product - utilizing something as a front end product means you're selling it for much less than what it's worth

in an attempt to produce a list of customers. A list of demonstrated customers is crucial because those individuals are more likely to purchase from you again. If they like what you had to provide the first time around then chances are they'll return for more.

Understanding how you'll utilize your audio product is very crucial.

Chapter 4:
Presenting The Product

Synopsis

A few individuals merely read the private label rights material word for word other people get more originative with the way they deliver their private label rights material audio product. Here are a few different ways you are able to deliver your info.

Get Creative

Carry out an interview

Have an acquaintance or relative question you about your subject. The idea here is to make you appear like an authority. Set up the questions beforehand and have your responses already made out. Make certain you keep it really professional and on subject.

As well you can interview someone else.

Having an authority record an audio interview is a really simple way to impress your customers. Experts may supply fantastic value to your product and offer supplementary insight on your subject.

Discover the experts on your subject. You are able to discover experts by executing a Google search for those who have sites on your subject or who are authoring articles about your subject.

Drop a line to the authority and invite an interview. Give a formal request to the authority explaining who you are, your site and subject, and why you'd like to interview him or her. Invite an audio interview, then cross your fingers and hope the reply is yes!

Make out the questions that you'd like your authority to answer. Take your time and produce sensible questions. You are able to even ask your customers for questions they'd like answered.

Send off the questions to the authority once he or she has agreed to be questioned. This will give your particular guest time to sufficiently prepare for the interview.

Arrange the particular date and hour for the interview.

Contact the authority the day before the interview to corroborate that his or her plans haven't shifted. Likewise confirm your meeting place if you're meeting in the flesh or which number you ought to utilize on the day of the interview.

Be on time! Telephone or arrive at the stipulatory time. Don't be late to the interview.

Carry on your interview in a professional fashion. Let the guest finish his or her sentences without disruptions. You might wish to ask follow-up questions to intriguing points the authority brings up.

Thank your guest verbally on audio and again after you've switched off your recording. Answer any queries your guest might have about where to discover and download your product.

Publish your product with the interview.

Produce a course

Turn your info into a course of study. Utilize the basic info as an introduction and then move into your other more innovative subjects. Depending upon the subject you pick out you are able to even think about assembling some kind of study guide or worksheets to put in with your audio product as an incentive.

Net courses may be every bit as good as traditional lectures, workshops, and independent learning, yet they've an added advantage: they enable both instructors and pupils to work according to their own optimal pace and agenda. Planning successful net courses, all the same, calls for educators to comprehend the differences---both honorable and not so great ---between real-time, face-to-face direction and the many variances of online course structure.

Realize that a successful net course calls for more than simply putting materials online and then expecting your pupils to teach themselves. Prompting pupils is challenging enough face-to-face; getting rid of personal interaction will doom the course to failure.

Formulate a clear-cut description of the course, including an intro or overview, goals and mileposts, and essentials or requirements. Produce a Frequently Asked Questions (FAQ) section that predicts queries pupils often have to avoid having your e-mail or user bulletin board flooded with requests for common info.

Get acquainted with available computer-based presentment and recording tools, both computer hardware and software packages, so that you are able to select those most advantageous based on substance and sort of interaction, and whether the course will be updated in the future or merely replaced. Learn how to utilize not just the instruction capacities of the programs but likewise the construction and customization capabilities.

Ascertain how you wish to deliver your course (e.g., audio, streaming audio, or in a self standing product with audio and transcripts). Once you formulate your course of study, produce it for the format in which it will be presented (and, more than likely, duplicated or recycled). For instance, you might present a product the initial time as a real-time live webinar with call-in chat, but record it as a downloadable audio.

Record and produce your presentation, recalling to refer to particular media or visuals, and adding pauses (or click commands) as essential. When you've the whole presentation in the proper format and in the suitable order, map the final contents to a timeline.

Change over files to a compressed format; upload the files to the suitable server or web site, and/or burn backup or distribution CDs.

Produce a series

A few subjects are best put together as a series rather than one hyper-long audio product. Split up the content. This will make it much simpler for your buyers to utilize it as a learning tool. It will likewise have a greater perceived value once you lay it out as a series.

Whether your customers are commuting, exercising or just don't feel like reading, audio books may be great for relaxation of amusement. Regrettably, a lot of audio books are distributed digitally as only a fistful of files, which may make navigating them tough. But you can give your customers what they are looking for by using free software that is available that lets you break your audio book into as few or as many files as you like. (We will cover tools in a later chapter)

Notice the times of where you wish your files to quit and begin.

Open your audio in Audacity, which is available on the net.

Pick out a time span by highlighting the audio wave shape. Utilize the corresponding time line above the waveform to pick out times for your edit.

Utilizing the File menu, pick out a format (MP3, WAV or OGG) to export.

Duplicate as required for additional cuts.

Feature a live session

If you're comfy enough you are able to present your product in a live session. Ask in everyone you know. Travel to assorted discussion boards and announce it so you are able to acquire a few listeners.

After you present the info invite the audience to ask questions.

Chapter 5:
Get The Correct Tools

Synopsis

In the past, I've never messing around too much with free software. Why, am I independently wealthy?

Nope, I was simply rather dissatisfied with the performance of the top notch software packages offered at that time, let alone free audio recording software. I was perpetually looking for improvements, hoping that computer programmers would finally "get" what the user wants.

But today things have changed.

A Closer Look At The Tools

Computers are quick enough to run even demanding audio applications and pro programs frequently provide more functions than you really require.

It's not that programmers bettered very much on the human user interface or the musical intelligence (in my modest opinion), but they've put through so many functions, that almost anything is possible for some reason. This makes software frequently more complicated than necessary for a particular task.

Consequently these days a different wish develops.

Recording software that has a devoted task, is easy to utilize and keeps you centered on your production idea.

This is where gratis music recording software enters.

There are a few awesome programs out there that give you all the sound quality and functions you require for a particular project. Occasionally even for free.

What's crucial today?

System requirements. Determine if the software is available for your operating system and if your PC is quick enough for this application. Manufacturer's recommendations are commonly set a bit too low. That means, find a better computer than suggested.

Audio caliber. You do not have to record on 64 bit/192kHz but you don't wish to record on 8 bit either. Your recording software package ought to at least support recording in CD caliber (16 bit/44.1кHz)

Low response time. If you wish to overdub (record, while you hear what's already recorded), you require a low latency interface with its drivers (ASIO, WMF, or interchangeable)

No severe Bugs. You don't want to lose one-half a day of recording work simply to discover that everything is gone simply because of a buggy software package. Take your time and try out the crucial functions on your own PC.

Software that does all you require. Yes, you might also need some recording functions, effects, headphone mix, MIDI functionality and so forth. Consider what you really require regarding your recording project and see, if the software supplies all these functions.

I surely don't wish to talk you into utilizing free software after you've invested into a big recording platform. I know the difference, however for beginners it's a good option. It's perhaps good enough to record your first hit product.

Free Software

This gratis music recording software is commonly easy to learn and not as feature clogged, that it takes weeks to research their functions.

But have a look for yourself. You are able to download and utilize these programs free of charge. Make your first steps into recording or

try them simply for fun to see, if these programs may make your life easier.

Kristal Audio Engine/Kreatives.com (PC)

A 16 channel multitrack recorder that bears ASIO, VST effects, up to 32 bit/192kHz Audio files and is simple to manage. This software ought to be enough for recording little projects except with all effects, filtering and mixing.

Audacity/Audacity (Mac/PC/Linux/BSD)

A quick free music editing software that's capable of multi-track recording for Linux, BSD, Mac OS, and Windows. Bears WAV, AIFF, Ogg, and MP3 formats. Characteristics include envelope editing, mixing, inbuilt effects and plug-ins, all with limitless undo. Regrettably no ASIO driver available because of legal troubles.

Freecorder

FreeCorder does precisely as the name suggests: it's an easy-to-use free software platform that lets you record sounds on your PC, whether that is a CD you're playing, Net streaming audio, games music, or a midi file. It:
Records what you hear from your speakers.
Saves recordings as MP3 files.
You are able to also record from the microphone or line-in inputs on your computer.

Quartz Audio Master

Quartz Audio Master is a gratis 4 audio track software program with a 16 track midi sequencer. Solely has delay, reverb, phaser and chorus but supports Quartz plug-ins. You are able to buy more audio tracks and it has excellent guides to learn how to utilize the software.

FREE Hi-Q Recorder

FREE Hi-Q Recorder records streaming audio, net radio, webcasts, music, meetings, classes, DVD sound, convert LP's, records, tapes and much more. It turnouts any sound source directly to MP3. The MP3 quality may be adjusted by selecting the Bitrate and stereo or mono. Hi-Q Recorder may also be used as a universal audio or video sound file converter.

The MP3-only format makes it of limited worth for serious recording, but ideal for podcasting and for utilization with iPods and other portable MP3 players.

Lame Encoder

Nowadays, LAME is considered the best MP3 encoder at mid-high bitrates and at VBR, by and large thanks to the dedicated work of its developers and the open source licensing model that let the project tap into engineering resources from all-round the world. Both caliber and speed improvements are still occurring, likely making LAME the only MP3 encoder still being actively developed.

Chapter 6:
Create The Transcript From PLR

Synopsis

An audio product that has a transcript included will sell for more than one that doesn't have a transcript included. Have you ever desired to purchase PLR, but hesitated as you were worried about duplicate material issues?

I empathize with how you feel. And I comprehend your skepticism. I'd feel the same way in your position.

Using PLR simply the way you got it may really affect your product rankings.

So what's the solution? As it turns out, there are many ways you are able to produce unique material utilizing PLR. Read on to learn more.

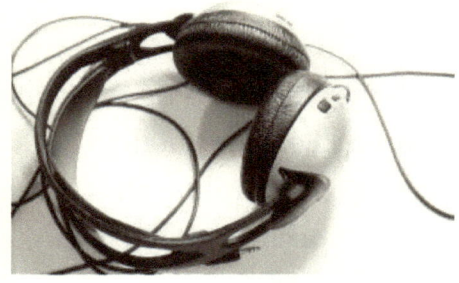

Tips For Transcripts

Blend two or more PLR report to produce unique material.

This one is simple. Simply take a portion from each report and put them together. Perhaps add a couple of sentences here and there to keep the flow fluid.

Combing material to create a unique content has an additional advantage that you are able to utilize this technique to produce more in-depth products.

Attempt to look for a basic theme. For instance, if you take material about Windows, some other about Mac, and yet some other about Linux, you are able to combine them and write content that gives an overview of all the assorted operating systems.

Break up material into longer material.

If you are able to combine material, you are able to split it too, correct?

Well, yes, technically. On the other hand you'll have to do a little writing of your own.

What you are able to do is take a paragraph or a thought from material and expand it into content in its own right. For instance, if you take material about the top 10 ways of executing something, you are able to likely write separate material for each of the techniques covered in the original material.

Calls for a bit of work, however hey, you wind up with more material than you started with.

Re-script the material (or get somebody else to do it).

If all your efforts at combining or splitting the material to produce unique content have bombed, the least you are able to do is merely rewrite all of the PLR material that you have.

Or if you don't wish to spend the time revising the material yourself, you are able to also outsource it to somebody else. Sites like elance give you access to numerous writers who may re-script your PLR material.

Translate to another language.

Who says your PLR material has to be utilized in the same language you bought it in? There are millions of individuals online whose native speech is something other than English. By translating your material in their language, you're not only producing unique material, but doing these individuals a great service.

Just make sure to ask a native speaker of the language to carry out the translation, and don't utilize some online tool for it, or your material will look and sound like gibberish!

Convert the material to audio, then back to text.

Simply put the material in front of you, begin recording, and continue reading the material. But rather than repeating what's in the material word for word, you are able to keep saying each sentence in another way than is composed.

You are able to even expand every sentence into stories or illustrations, and add your own position here and there.

When you've finished recording, you'll be able to transcribe it back and acquire a text version. If you're too lazy to type, or don't have the time, you are able to use one of the transcribing services online or a voice to text program.

Wrapping Up

If you've been surfing the net lately, you likely noticed that audio is cropping up everyplace you look. It's showing up as info products, audio testimonials on sites, teleconferences, audio postcards in e-mail, etc.

Remember what you'll need to begin creating some killer audios:

Well, the obvious resources are a mic, software, and a sound card. The not so perceptible things are hard drive space and the power to run the software package.

Net marketers trust in the adage that the audio visual world is absolutely more appealing than the written one. It's obvious that the whole concept of marketing will look more toward utilizing such mechanisms effectively to push the sites and better their profitability.

While there's no doubt that audio and videos are the largest ploys to draw in traffic to your site, it's of import to discover just how to plan and execute audio, so that it maximizes your product.

It's equally crucial to add zing and flavor to your product by ensuring that you produce pleasing audio, accompanied by the correct sort of music for some products. It's crucial that the music you utilize or produce appeals to all ages and has a particular connection with your company.

Entertainment and info are the 2 main aspects involved in producing audio for your product.

Emotions are a really crucial aspect, which ought to be exploited while utilizing audio. A really simple and aboveboard example of tapping emotions is the audio visual ads that are commonly viewed on TV. Utilizing the same principles, you are able to produce your own audio product, which appeal to the emotional side of people.

Hopefully this guide has given you valuable tools to begin your winning audio product.

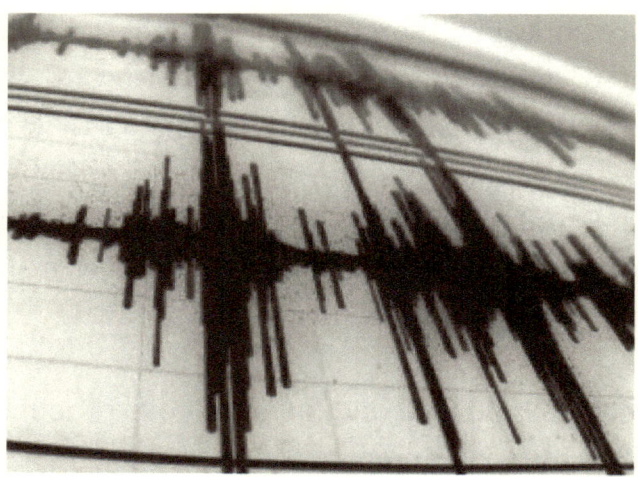

A different advantage is that audio content is really easy to produce. . You are able to even utilize free audio software to produce this stuff. But you are able to also buy professional audio recording software. As a matter of fact all you need to do is to buy a great microphone and hook it into your home computer. Then you are almost ready to record your money making audios. Naturally it's advisable to compose a script of your message beforehand.

Audio Ads

Everybody is beginning to comprehend the impact Net networks will have on TV and cable, more significantly, marketing. As a matter of fact, that affect has already started making itself obvious as TV ads and commercials lose their efficacy due to the shift that individuals are making.

Lots of individuals are already online day-after-day whether for work or school, due to its immense amount of data. It only adds up that they're getting familiar with and attached to the activities net.

Ad campaigners and marketers have had to develop in order to keep their products successful and their companies going. Millions of marketing, ad and entertainment careers may be affected by this direct shift to the way consumers relax.

Why advertizing is shifting!

Cyberspace hasn't just altered what individuals do for entertainment; it has likewise changed the way consumers shop. This is why it's

www.ingramcontent.com/pod-product-compliance
Lightning Source LLC
Chambersburg PA
CBHW030537220526
45463CB00007B/2867

www.ingramcontent.com/pod-product-compliance
Lightning Source LLC
Chambersburg PA
CBHW030547220526
45463CB00007B/3013